Embroidery for Group Working

Christine Andrews

with

Vera Bradshaw
Mab Driver

Doreen Holt
Jean Parry
Joan Thatcher

Molly Taylor
Jane Wood

Dryad Press Ltd
LONDON

ISBN 0 8521 9641 5

Typeset by Chelmsford Origination Limited, Chelmsford, Essex
and printed in Great Britain by
Anchor Brendon Ltd, Tiptree, Essex
for the publishers
Dryad Press Limited,
4 Fitzhardinge Street
London W1H 0AH

Contents

Acknowledgment

I would like to thank all the people who helped and encouraged me in the writing of this book. In particular, seven members of the Berkshire Branch of the Embroiderers' Guild namely Vera Bradshaw, Mab Driver, Doreen Holt, Jean Parry, Joan Thatcher, Molly Taylor and Jane Wood who joined me in this project at the beginning and remained with me, contributing their invaluable expertise, until the final pages were completed. I am also indebted to the Berkshire Branch for allowing me to include a photograph of their beautiful table cloth showing the combined work of the members in the colourful border of log cabin patchwork squares.

Warmest thanks go: to the Bucklebury Hall Committee for permitting me to photograph the tympanum in the village hall and for allowing me to include the illustration as a fine example of group working; to Jan Messent for her superb drawings and diagrams; and to Ray Hebron for the photographs for this book.

Finally I do not forget the forbearance shown by my sister Gwenda during the writing of this book. A talented artist herself, she has always shown great interest in my embroidery designs.

Foreword

It is with pleasure that I write the foreword to this book, as I know all the contributors personally, having been connected with the Berkshire Branch of the Embroiderers' Guild for many years.

Christine Andrews and the seven other members of the Branch have been working together as a group on this project for two years, and know from their experience how rewarding such joint activities can be. I know that they will have been most caring to ensure that details of the project are accurate.

Accepting the challenge for a group project can be daunting but sharing the problems that might arise helps to overcome any difficulties.

I hope that the valuable experience gained from the suggestions in this book will enable the less confident workers to go on to develop their own ideas.

Jan Beaney

Introduction

Students new to the craft of embroidery often find the thought of embarking on an elaborate project rather daunting. It is, of course, a very time-consuming craft and requires great concentration and painstaking attention to detail.

Consequently, the division of projects into parts enables a number of individuals to take part in the production of a far more intricate venture than they would normally contemplate. An added incentive is that the worker will see the finished and assembled piece within a relatively short period of time.

Group working provides the perfect opportunity to learn from other people's experiences. Apart from being able to help each other when problems occur, members of the group can contribute to discussions on the subjects of colouring, stitches, threads and background design; all of which are vital to the completion of the project.

There is a great team spirit involved in the working of each project whether it is done to earn pin money, as occupational therapy, or simply for fun.

The aim of this book is to stimulate and provide ideas for teachers of courses who have students of varying ability.

Section One

Cushions

HEXAGONAL PATCHWORK CUSHION 30 cm (12 in.) SQUARE
(colour plate 1 and figs. 4 and 5)

MATERIALS

46 cm (½ yd) of plain cotton fabric 91 cm (36 in.) wide
23 cm (¼ yd) of patterned cotton fabric 91 cm (36 in.) wide
23 cm (¼ yd) of plain cotton fabric to tone with patterned fabric
30 cm (12 in.) square cushion pad
5 cm (2 in.) hexagonal template with 'window'
Stiff paper for shapes

METHOD

1. Using the paper and template cut 45 full hexagonal and 21 half hexagonal shapes.
2. Cut 45 hexagonal shapes in a selection of patterned and plain fabrics to make a pattern, and 21 half hexagonal shapes in plain fabric for the spaces along the sides (fig. 1).
(N.B. Leave 6 mm (¼ in.) turnings on all sides of the fabric shapes, and use the 'window' to place any motif in the centre (fig. 2)).
3. With paper shape on the wrong side of fabric, turn over 6 mm (¼ in.) allowed and tack.
4. Join all the patches by oversewing the edges, right sides together, to form the chosen design (figs. 3 and 4). When the design is completed, remove the paper shapes and press.

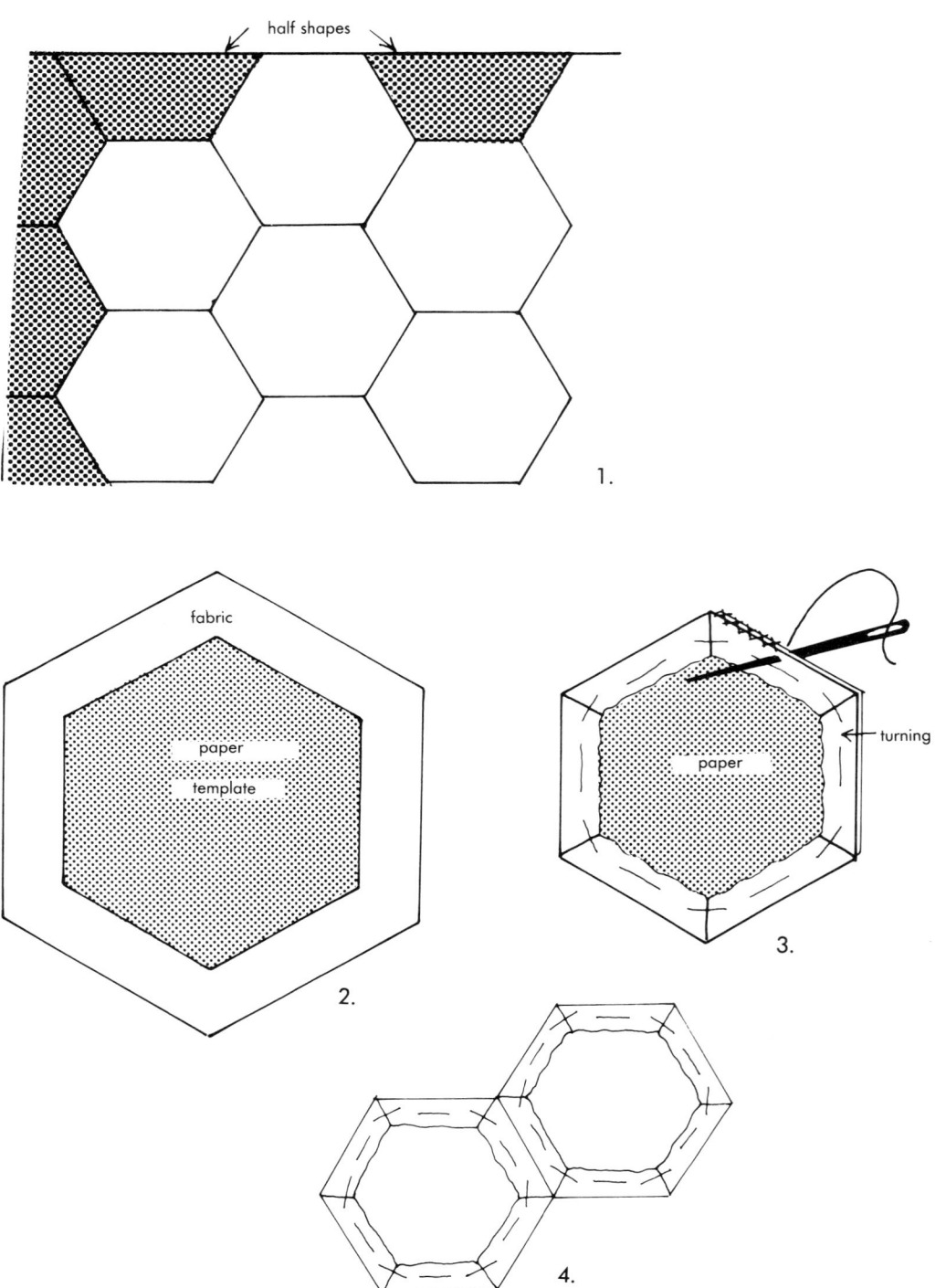

half shapes

1.

fabric

paper
template

2.

paper

turning

3.

4.

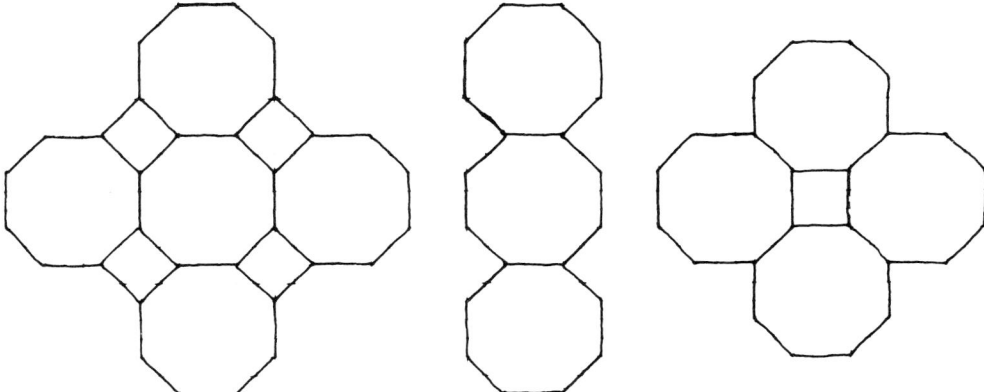

5. Designs using octagons and squares

ASSEMBLING THE CUSHION

1.   From the 46 cm (½ yd) of plain fabric cut a piece 30 cm x 30 cm (12 in. x 12 in.) for the backing. Place this, right sides together, with the patchwork and stitch round three sides, 6 mm (¼ in.) from edges.

2.   Trim, turn inside out and poke out the corners.

3.   Put the cushion pad inside, turn in the top edges of the backing and the patchwork, oversewing along the edge.

N.B. Never press patchwork with the tacking stitches still in place as they will leave marks.

Variation: Use octagonal-shaped templates for a slightly more adventurous design, (see fig. 5).

LOG CABIN PATCHWORK CUSHION 41 cm (16 in.) SQUARE
(colour plate 1 and fig. 6)

Log cabin patchwork is ideal for group work, so long as a hot iron is readily available, this is because the work needs constant pressing as it progresses. It can be stitched by hand or machined, the latter giving good practice for straight stitching on short lengths. The cushion illustrated is made from 10 cm x 10 cm (4 in. x 4 in.) squares joined together to form the 41 cm (16 in.) cushion.

MATERIALS

4 pieces of calico 11 cm (4 ½ in.) square
Lengths of harmonising dark and light shades of fabric 3 cm (1 in.) wide
1 piece of toning fabric 3.8 cm (1½ in.) square for centre
Backing fabric 46 cm x 91 cm (18 in. x 36 in.)
41 cm (16 in.) square cushion pad

METHOD

1. On the 11cm (4½ in.) square of calico draw diagonals to find the centre and from this draw lines 13 mm (½ in.) apart to all sides to form a grid of 13 mm (½ in.) squares (fig. 6A). This grid will enable the stitching of each 'log' to be straight and the same width throughout.
2. Over the centre mark place the 4 cm (1½ in.) square and tack (fig. 6A).
3. With the right sides together place one light coloured strip to the right of the square and stitch 6 mm (¼ in.) from the edge of the centre square, using the grid lines as a guide (fig. 6B). Fold back and press.
4. Stitch another light strip at right-angles along the bottom to overlap the first strip in the same way (fig. 6C). Place a dark strip at right-angles to the second light strip (fig. 6D) and then another dark strip at right-angles to this one (fig. 6E).
5. One square is now complete (fig. 6E).
6. Continue, keeping the light strips on one side and the dark on the opposite until there are three strips from the centre square on all four sides (fig. 6F).
7. Press flat and when all four squares are complete, stitch along the outside grid line of two patches and then the other two. Join the two pairs together so that either dark or light shades form a pattern at the centre.

ASSEMBLING THE CUSHION

1. Cut the backing piece of fabric into half lengthwise and make a 3 cm (1 in.) hem on one side of each.
2. On the right side of one half tack the completed 41 cm (16 in.) log cabin square.
3. Stitch with zigzag machining or stitch by hand.
4. Make a French seam along the three unhemmed sides.
5. Turn inside out, poke out the corners, put in the 41 cm (16 in.) cushion pad and oversew along the top edge.
(N.B. The cushion pads should always be a tight fit to make a full cushion.)

. Patchwork cushions; two made with hexagonal units and two
ade with log cabin units.

. Wall hangings made using letters in cross stitch on canvas.

. Waste bins worked in separate sections.

. Place mats with separately-worked designs applied to them.

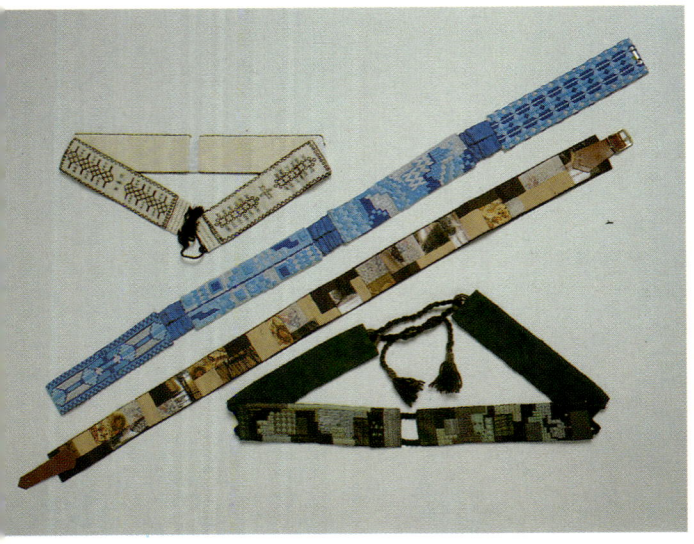

5. Belts worked in different types of embroidery showing various fastenings and methods of joining sections.

6. Child's waistcoat made from a 'fabric' assembled from patchwork squares.

7. Collection of Dorset buttons, tassels, plaits and bobbles.

8. Gardening apron made of denim or sailcloth fabric showing five separately-embroidered pockets.

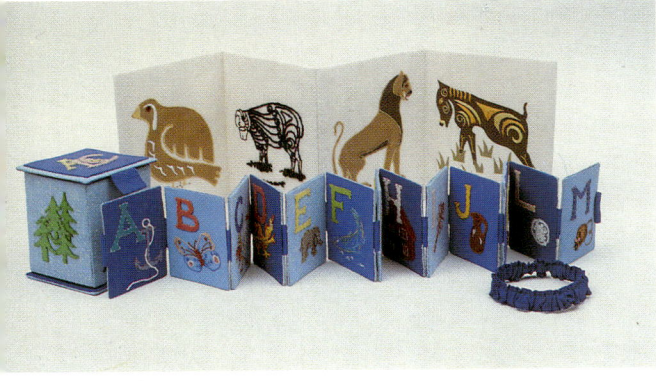

9. Animals in patchwork squares; dog family, dog mobile and snakes.

10. Patchwork clowns made from diamond units and jumping clown made from Suffolk puffs.

11. Standing alphabet decorated with motifs and appliquéd letters and child's animal book.

12. Pram or cot quilts made using separately embroidered panels applied before the whole is quilted.

13. Child's measuring chart showing motifs worked separately. The rhymes can be printed or embroidered on tape or ribbon and added to each motif, or sewn to the back.

14. Tablecloth belonging to the Berkshire Branch of the Embroiderers' Guild. Log cabin units were worked by members and applied to the cloth by machine stitching.

15. Tablecloth worked by members of the Bucklebury and Marlston Women's Institute showing the various activities of the Institute.

16. The tympanum above the stage of the Bucklebury Village Hall illustrating the history of the village. The designs were worked on iron-on Vilene backing, then assembled and applied to the backcloth.

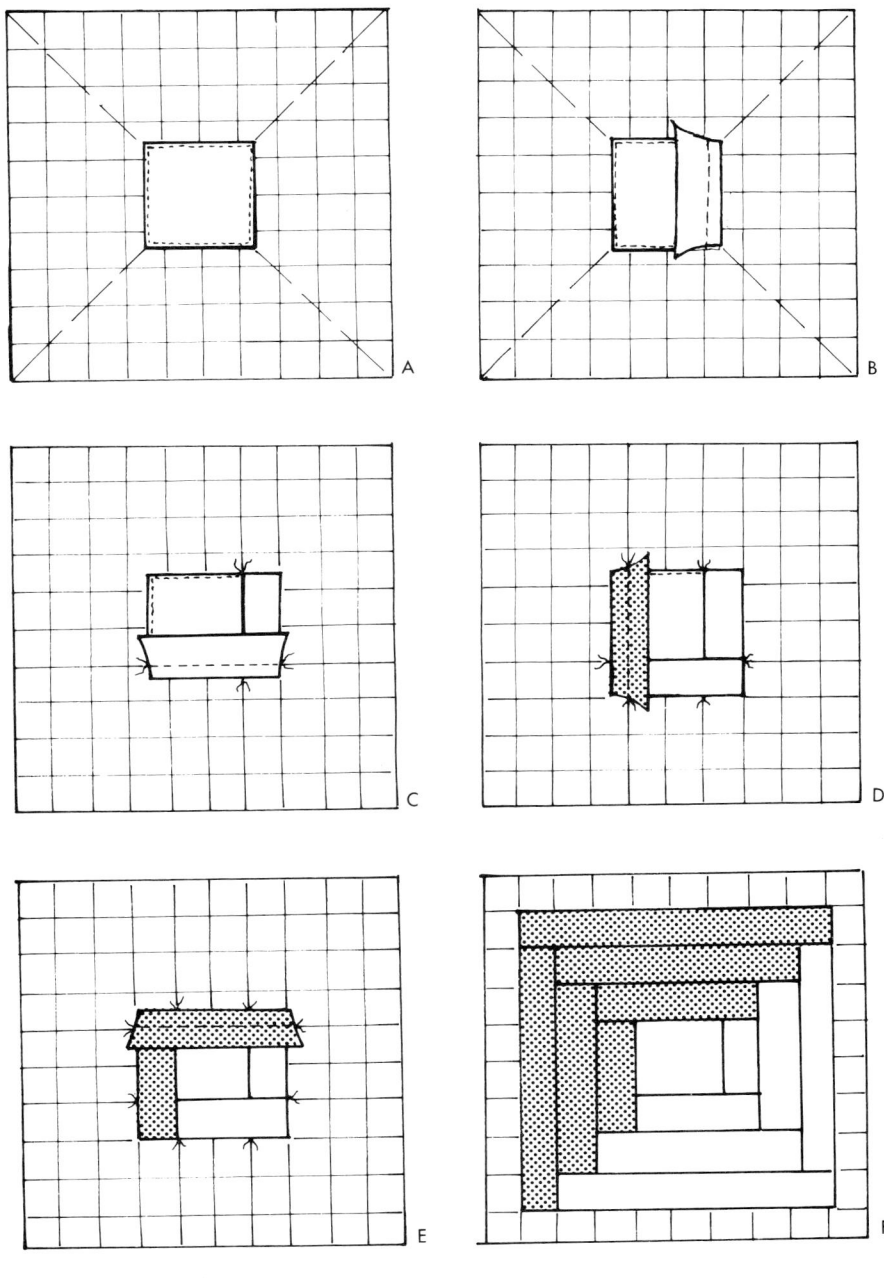

Finger Plates *(figs. 7 and 8)*

Almost any type of embroidery can be used for these finger plates. Clear pieces of thick plastic with screw holes and bevelled edges are obtainable from hardware stores. Clear plastic can also be bought in sheets and cut to the required size. Those illustrated measure 30 cm x 8 cm (12 in. x 3 in.)

MATERIALS

Clear plastic cut to 30 cm x 8 cm (12 in. x 3 in.)
1 piece of strong card 30 cm x 8 cm (12 in. x 3 in.)
Fabric, preferably linen, to cut 3 pieces each measuring 10 cm x 13 cm (4 in. x 5 in.)
Embroidery threads to suit fabric and design
1 piece of pelmet Vilene 30 cm x 8 cm (12 in. x 3 in.) for backing

METHOD

1. Mark 13 mm (½ in.) in from all edges of each of the three pieces.
2. Work an embroidery of your choice on each piece well inside the top and two sides of the 13 mm (½ in.) mark, (fig. 8A).
3. When finished, place the three pieces top to bottom and join across the 13 mm (½ in.) fold marks (fig. 8B).
4. Embroider across the join and, if possible, work a continuing line of the designs.
5. Place the three joined sections over the card using the 13 mm (½ in.) allowance and lace at the back in both directions (fig. 8C).
6. Stitch the pelmet Vilene to the panel by neat oversewing. It is now ready to be inserted behind the plastic and screwed to the door.

Wall Hangings *(colour plate 2)*

Projects such as wall hangings which can be separated into individual pieces are ideal for group work. Designs can be made using letters of the alphabet, bird or flower shapes or even chart diagrams from knitting patterns. Plastic canvas is easy to use and needs no turnings or neatening.

MATERIALS

8 cm (3 in.) squares of canvas
8 cm (3 in.) squares of pelmet Vilene
White and coloured 4-ply wool in toning shades
1 ball of metallic-style thread
69 cm (¾ yd) of satin or velvet ribbon 4 cm (1½ in.) wide

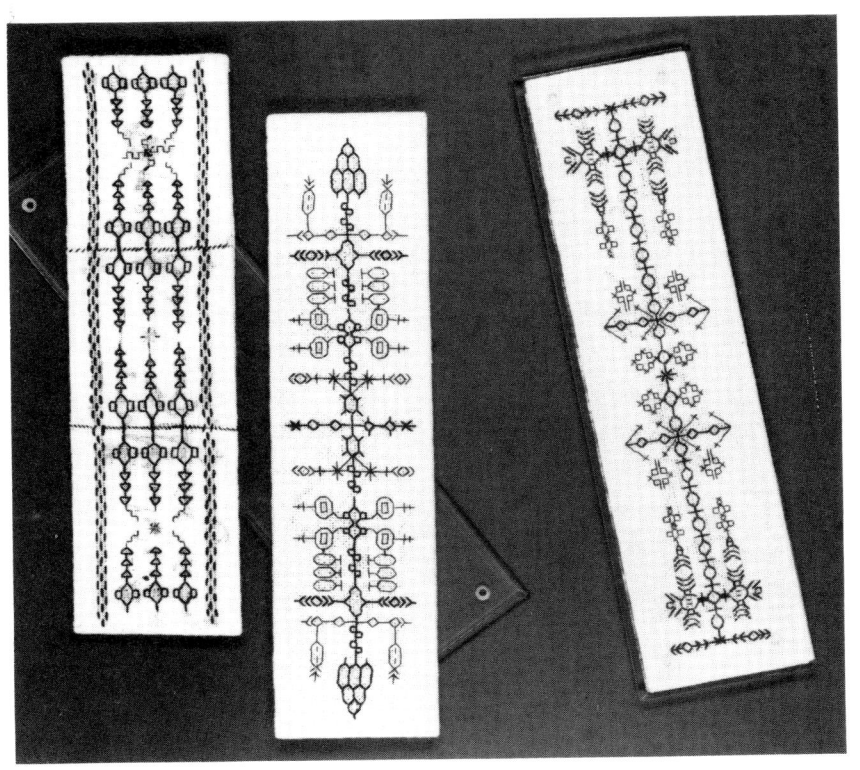

7.

A.   B.   C.

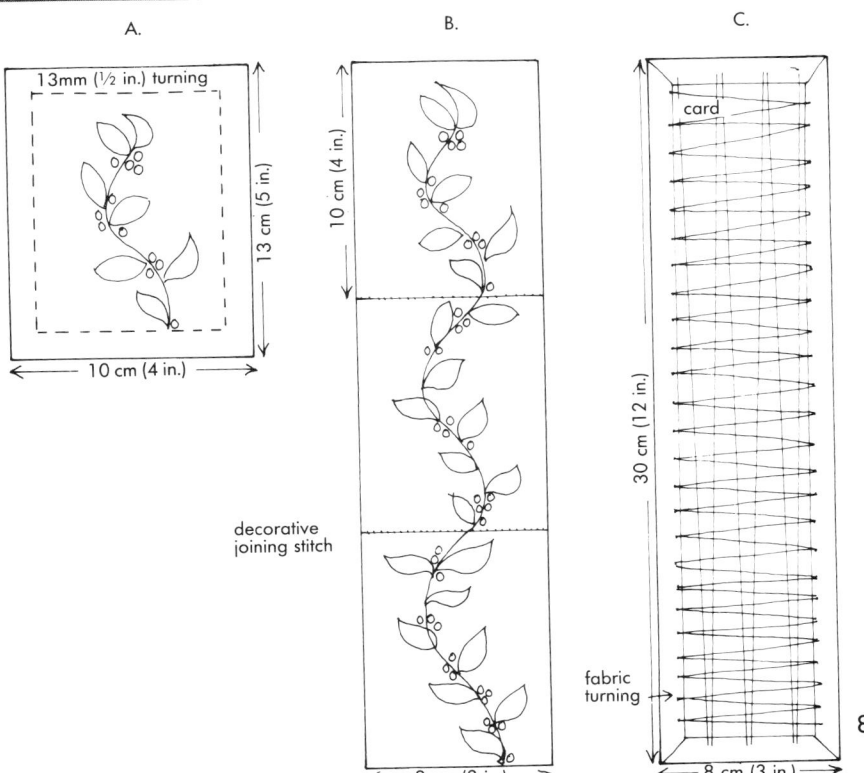

A.

13mm (½ in.) turning

13 cm (5 in.)

10 cm (4 in.)

B.

10 cm (4 in.)

decorative joining stitch

8 cm (3 in.)

C.

card

30 cm (12 in.)

fabric turning

8 cm (3 in.)

8.

15

METHOD

The illustrated squares are worked in tent stitch (fig. 9). Other stitches could be used to vary the texture.

1.   For each square select the letter to be used and, following the squared paper design, outline it in tent stitch using the metallic-style thread.
2.   Fill in the centre of each letter with coloured wool.
3.   Complete the square by filling in the background with white wool.
4.   Overstitch the edges of each square with the metallic-style thread.
5.   Stitch the squares of pelmet Vilene to the back of each worked square.
6.   Space the squares along the ribbon, making a loop at the top for hanging and an inverted V at the end to prevent fraying.
7.   Stitch the ribbon to the Vilene at the top and bottom of each square.

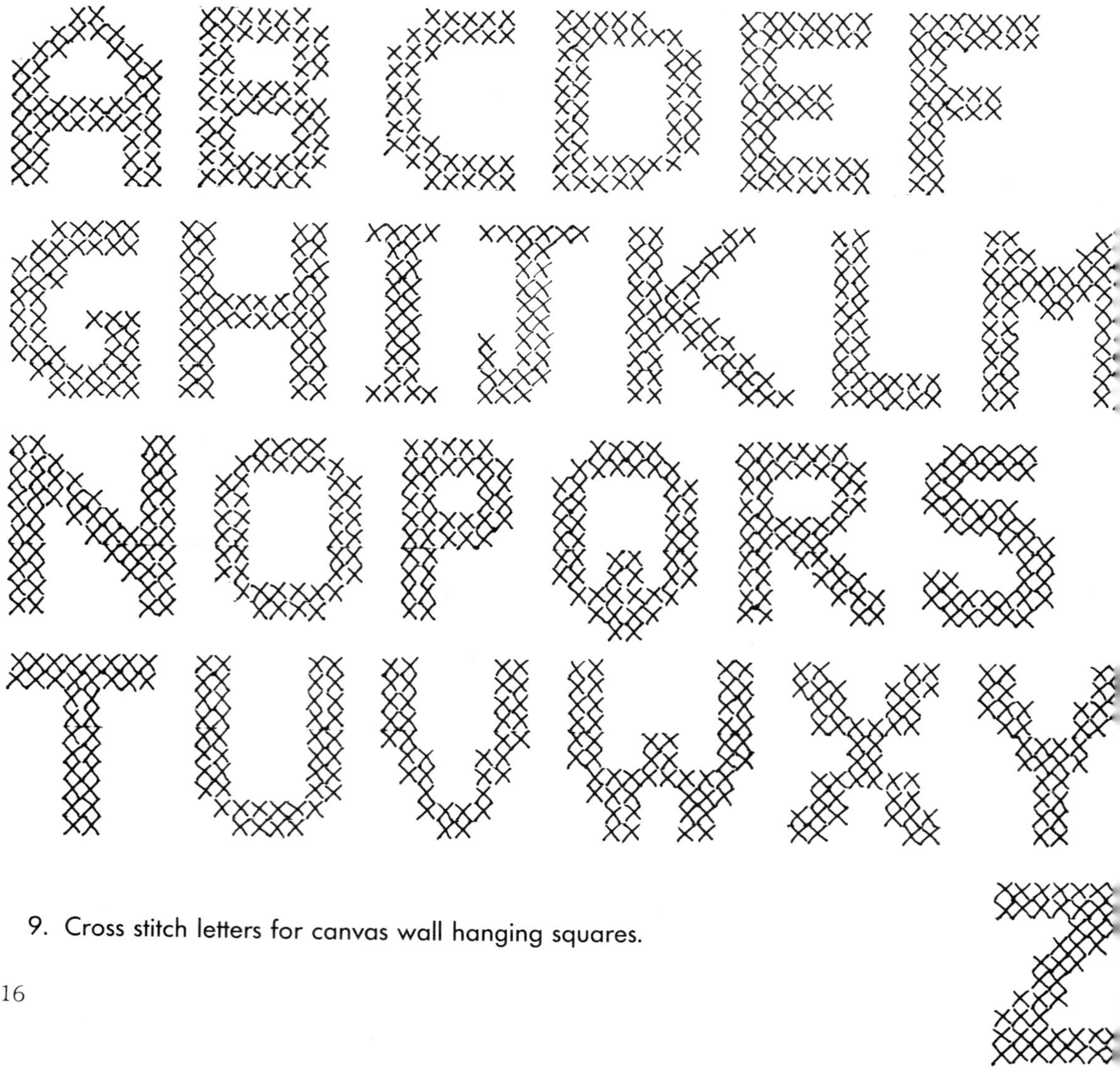

9. Cross stitch letters for canvas wall hanging squares.

Waste Bins *(colour plate 3 and fig. 10)*

The type of embroidery used for this project will be dictated by the design of the room the bin is for. The bins illustrated are worked in patchwork and canvaswork and are made from the tins obtained from a catering service. Each measures 18 cm (7 in.) high by 15 cm (6 in.) diameter but other sizes can be used and the embroidered sections adjusted to suit the shape and the number of people working in the group.

THE PATCHWORK BIN

MATERIALS

1 tin 18 cm (7 in.) high and 15 cm (6 in.) diameter, painted white inside
Pieces of harmonising fabrics for the patchwork
697 cm (3 yds) of 3 cm (1 in.) wide bias binding to tone, cut into 4 x 20 cm (8 in.) lengths and 2 x 56 cm (22 in.) lengths
1 piece of card 15 cm (6 in.) diameter
Toning fabric to cover card
61 cm (24 in.) of white adhesive tape
Adhesive

METHOD

1. Draw on squared paper a rectangle 18 cm x 14 cm (7 in. x 5½ in.) and divide this into squares and oblongs and number each ready for the patchwork (fig. 10A).
2. Make four copies of this numbered design. Keep the original as a reference and cut the others up as templates for the patchwork sections.
3. Cover the paper templates with fabric and join in the pattern to make four sections.
4. When all are completed, test for size round the tin and join together in a tube, covering the long edges with the 3 cm (1 in.) binding, zigzag stitching over the patchwork (fig. 10B).
5. Stitch with zigzag, along the top and bottom of the patchwork tube.
6. Tuck the bottom edge of the bias strip under the tin base and stick.
7. Cover the 15 cm (6 in.) circle of card with fabric, adjusting the size if necessary and lace across back (fig. 10C). Fit and stick to the base of tin.
8. Tuck the top edge of the bias binding over the tin edge at the top and with the adhesive tape attach it to the inside of the tin (fig. 10B).

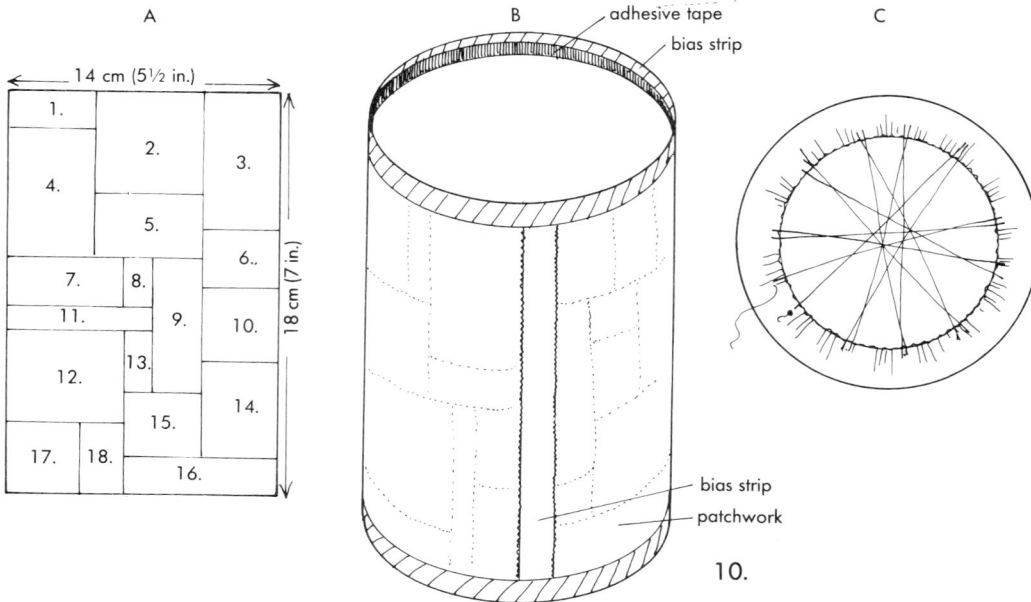

A   14 cm (5½ in.)

B   adhesive tape   bias strip

18 cm (7 in.)

bias strip
patchwork

10.

C

Tray cloths and place mats of all shapes can be worked in sections, providing that the joints are perfectly flat (fig. 11 and 12 (right)).

Circular Tray Cloth

MATERIALS

46 cm (½ yd) of linen or pre-shrunk cotton fabric 91 cm (36 in.) wide
Embroidery threads
Bias binding 13 mm (½ in.) wide to match fabric
Ric-rac braid

METHOD

1. Cut out a circle of fabric 46 cm (18 in.) diameter and divide into quarters.
2. Make a 13 mm (½ in.) turning on the wrong side of fabric all round each section and slip stitch bias binding over turning to make a flat 'hem' (fig. 12A).
3. Work selected design on each segment.
4. Oversew each finished segment together on the wrong side, so that a circular mat is formed (fig. 12B).
5. Edge the right side with ric-rac braid, holding it down with a decorative stitch to harmonise with the embroidery (fig. 12C).
6. Work a star motif at the centre join (fig. 12D).

11.

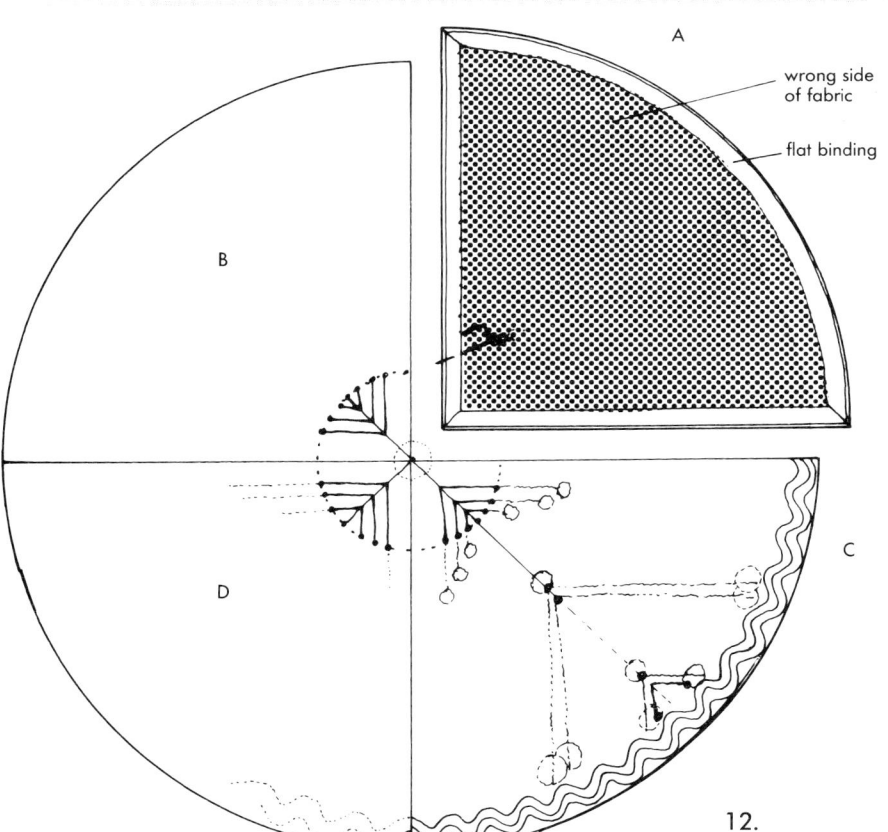

A

wrong side
of fabric

flat binding

B

C

D

12.

Rectangular Place Mats
(colour plate 4 and fig. 13)

MATERIALS FOR BOTH PLACE MATS

1 piece of background fabric 43 cm x 36 cm (17 in. x 14 in.)
1 piece of backing fabric 43 cm x 36 cm (17 in. x 14 in.)
2 pieces of plain linen-type fabric 10 cm x 28 cm (4 in. x 11 in.) for the embroidery panels
1 piece of pelmet Vilene 42 cm x 34 cm (16½ in. x 13½ in.) if desired

METHOD FOR PLACE MAT 1 (fig. 13A)

1. Make 13 mm (½ in.) turnings on the wrong side all round each small piece of fabric.
2. Draw or trace, then work a design or motif to occupy most of the space on each of the small panels.
3. Make 13 mm (½ in.) turnings all round on the wrong side of the background and backing fabric.
4. Place and tack these two embroidered panels on to the background fabric, equidistant from the top and bottom (fig. 13A).
5. Attach the panels with an embroidery stitch.
6. With the 13 mm (½ in.) turnings inside, tack and machine the background and backing fabrics together.

METHOD FOR PLACE MAT 2 *(fig. 13B)*

1. As for place mat 1
2. As for place mat 1
3. As for place mat 1
4. Arrange four embroidered pieces, having made 13 mm (½ in.) turnings on the wrong side on all of them.
5. Join these together with slip stitches or an embroidery stitch making sure that the centre join is accurate.
6. Back the four joined pieces to the backing fabric as for place mat 1.
(A piece of pelmet Vilene inserted between the two pieces of fabric before machining will give added thickness.)

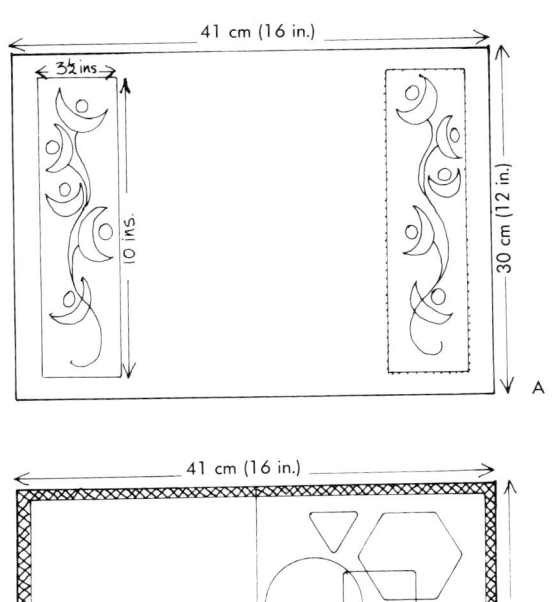

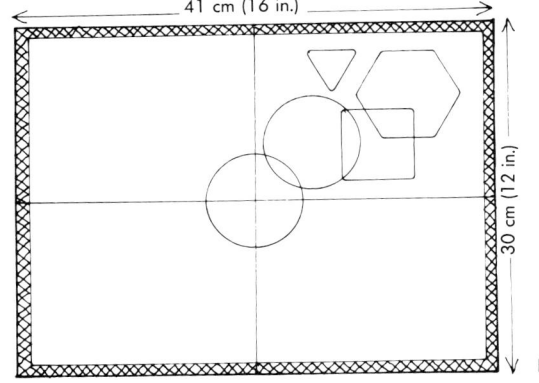

13.

Knee-Pad Blotter *(fig. 14)*

This blotter is very useful as a knee-pad when writing letters in bed or in an awkward chair. It needs only odd lengths of canvas and wools.

MATERIALS

2 pieces of canvas (14 or 16 holes to the inch) 5 cm x 24 cm (2 in. x 9½ in.)
Skeins of crewel wool, or any non-fluffing yarn which will fill the holes of the canvas easily
Tapestry needle no. 21
Mounting card 33 cm x 24 cm (13 in. x 9½ in.)
Piece of felt to harmonise with the embroidery 33 cm x 24 cm (13 in. x 9½ in.)
Blotting paper 33 cm x 24 cm (13 in. x 9½ in.)
Strong thread for lacing at back
Adhesive suitable for fabric and card

METHOD

1. Leaving a multiple of four canvas holes in both directions, turn over the excess canvas on all four sides and buttonhole stitch all round through both thicknesses in the main colour to give a firm edge.

2. Work a pattern in multiples of four holes using harmonising colours to fill both pieces of canvas (fig. 14A, B, C and D).

3. When both pieces are complete, place on to card at each end and lace from top to bottom firmly.

4. Lace canvas at back from side to side so that canvas and card are both firm (fig. 14E).

5. Glue the felt to the card to cover the lacing and stitch the embroidered canvas to the felt at the top, side and bottom.

6. Trim the blotting paper to fit and insert between canvas strips and card.

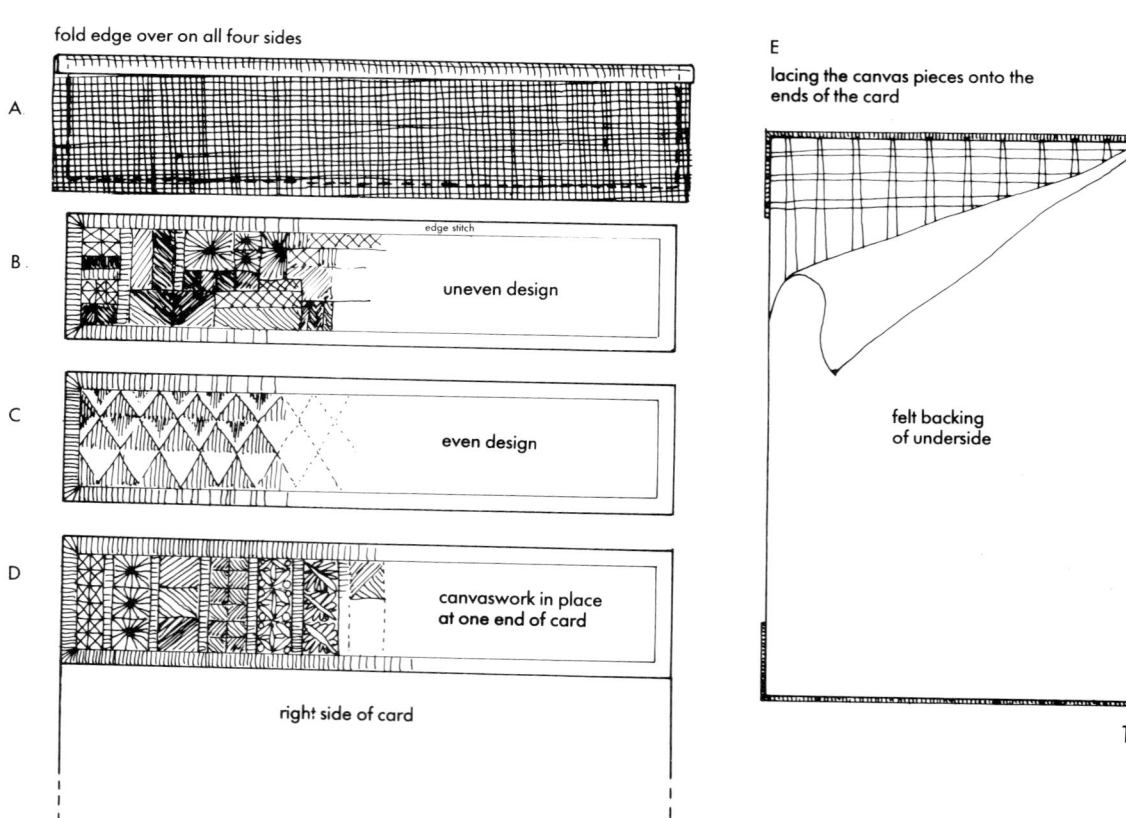

fold edge over on all four sides

A

edge stitch

B.   uneven design

C   even design

D   canvaswork in place at one end of card

right side of card

E

lacing the canvas pieces onto the ends of the card

felt backing of underside

1

Section Two

Belts *(figs. 15 and 16)*

Belts are an excellent way of using group work, as each belt can be divided into squares and oblongs before being worked in the chosen type of embroidery. The sections can then be backed and stitched to form a continuous strip (fig. 15). Belts also use up odd lengths of canvas and fabrics. Each belt illustrated measures 86 cm (34 in.) when fully stretched. Different sizes can be made by working a different number of sections to suit the group.

A variety of connections and different types of fastenings for joining the sections is shown; all are interchangeable.

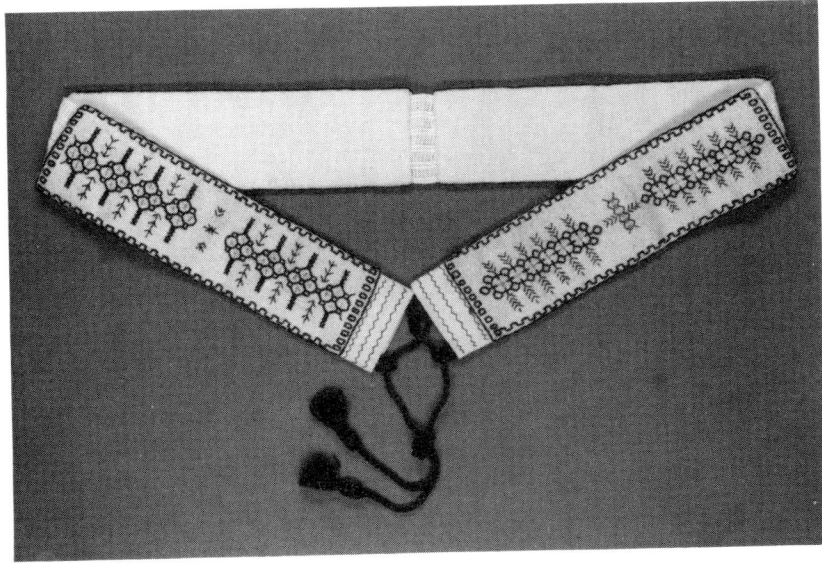

15.

MATERIALS FOR CANVAS BELT *(fig. 16A)*

4 pieces of canvas (14 or 16 holes to the inch) 22 cm x 6 cm (8½ in. x 2½ in.)
91 cm (1 yd) Petersham ribbon 5 cm (2 in.) wide
13 mm (½ in.) wide elastic
Thin material 11 cm (4½ in.) to match embroidery for covering elastic
Wools to harmonise in colour and thickness
Tapestry needle no. 20
Strap and buckle for fastening
Adhesive tape or tacking cotton

METHOD

1. Bind with adhesive tape or oversew the four pieces of canvas 6 mm (¼ in.) from the edge all round.
2. Work canvas stitches to form patterns on each section leaving the 6 mm (¼ in.) spare all round.
3. Remove tape, if used, and turn in all edges to make the section measure 20 cm x 5 cm (8 in. x 2 in.).
4. Cut four pieces of Petersham ribbon 22 cm (8½ in.) long. Oversew these on the wrong side of each finished canvas section along the long edges. Turn in the short ends but do not sew.
5. Cut 6 x 6 cm (2½ in.) lengths elastic and cover each with a 'tube' made from the thin fabric measuring 10 cm x 4 cm (4 in. x 1½ in.) so that it will gather along the unstretched elastic between the sections as shown in (A).
6. Insert two of these covered pieces of elastic into each of the unsewn ends of the canvas sections and stitch very securely. Neaten the unsewn parts at the ends. This will join all the sections into a continuous belt leaving the two extreme ends empty.
7. Into these ends insert the strap and buckle parts of the fastening.
N.B. Any of the other methods of joining the sections may be used as in fig. 16B using waist elastic and fig. 16C using two lengths of cord threaded right through the belt sections with adjustable spaces left between the sections, or oversewing the sections and leaving no gaps at all (fig. 16D).
Each section could also be worked in blackwork (see finger plates); or canvaswork (see waste bins or knee-pad blotter); or in geometrical patchwork (see waste bins).

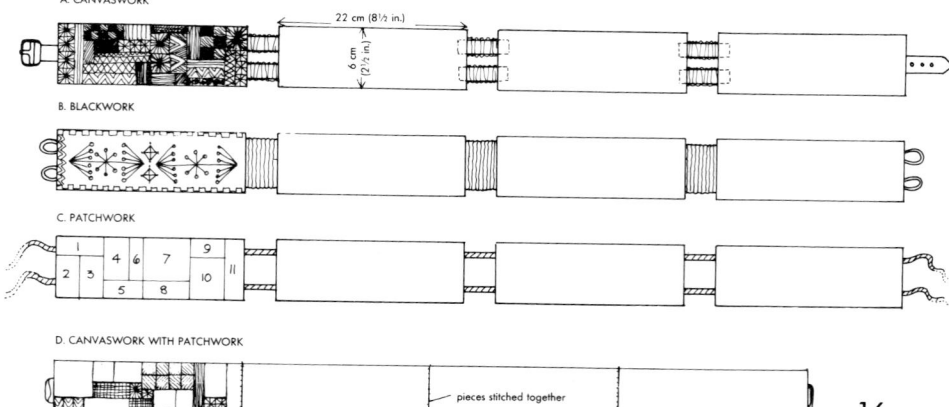

A. CANVASWORK

22 cm (8½ in.)

6 cm (2½ in.)

B. BLACKWORK

C. PATCHWORK

D. CANVASWORK WITH PATCHWORK

pieces stitched together

16.

Child's Patchwork Waistcoat
(colour plate 6 and fig. 17)

MATERIALS (to fit up to 76 cm (30 in.) chest)

15 cm (6 in.) of 91 cm (36 in.) wide fabric in six different prints to tone
51 cm (20 in.) of 91 cm (36 in.) wide lining fabric
51 cm (20 in.) of 91 cm (36 in.) wide polyester 57 g (2 oz) wadding
Fabric or cord for tie fastening, or hooks & eyes or buttons & loops
Squared dressmaking paper or brown paper for pattern
Paper for templates

METHOD

The easiest way to make this waistcoat is to make a complete piece of fabric from the made-up patchwork squares and cut the waistcoat shape from it.

To make the complete piece, 153 squares are needed:
24 x A, 23 x B, 22 x C, 22 x D, 24 x E and 24 x F.

1. Cut all the 5 cm (2 in.) squares of paper and cover each with fabric cut 7 cm x 7 cm (2¾ in. x 2¾ in.) allowing 1 cm (⅜ in.) turnings all round.
2. When all the squares are completed decide on the layout and then sew the patches together in strips.
3. Matching the edges carefully, machine or handsew these strips together to form the fabric.
4. Press and lay on the paper pattern of the waistcoat and cut out. Also cut out the waistcoat shape in lining fabric and polyester wadding.
5. Tack wadding to the wrong side of the lining piece.
6. With right side of lining to right side of patchwork, tack and machine 1 cm (⅜ in.) from all edges, leaving a 15 cm (6 in.) opening along the bottom.
7. Turn inside out, slipstitch along this opening and handsew the shoulder fronts to the back.
8. Add chosen fastenings.

shoulder — shoulder

A	E	B	F	C	D	A	E	B	E	A	D	C	F	B	E	A
F	C	D	A	E	B	F	C	D	C	F	B	E	A	D	C	F
A	E	B	F	C	D	A	E	B	E	A	D	C	F	B	E	A
F	C	D	A	E	B	F	C	D	C	F	B	E	A	D	C	F
A	E	B	F	C	D	A	E	B	E	A	D	C	F	B	E	A
F	C	D	A	E	B	F	C	D	C	F	B	E	A	D	C	F
A	E	B	F	C	D	A	E	B	E	A	D	C	F	B	E	A
F	C	D	A	E	B	F	C	D	C	F	B	E	A	D	C	F
A	E	B	F	C	D	A	E	B	E	A	D	C	F	B	E	A

centre back

17.

Dorset Buttons and Pendants

(colour plate 7 and fig. 18)

Handmade buttons add distinction to clothing or accessories and can be made individually or in matching groups. Similarly brooches, pendants and necklaces can be made to tone with outfits. These can be made by using larger rings or by forming the smaller buttons into hanging shapes or by threading them into a length.

MATERIALS

Rustproof rings the desired size
Threads, strong cottons, wools, silks, fine ribbon or metallic threads
Crewel needles

METHOD

1.   Tightly work close buttonhole stitch all round the ring and fasten off securely (fig. 18A).
2.   Push the outside edges of the stitches to the inside of the ring (fig. 18B).
3.   Using a long thread, wrap tightly across the centre of ring (back and front) and continue winding in equal sections round the ring to give 12 spokes (fig. 18C).
4.   Thread a crewel needle with the remaining end and catch the spokes together at the hub of the wheel with two cross stitches to secure (fig. 18D).
5.   Starting from the centre-back, bring the thread through and work back-stitches round the spokes packing them firmly until the whole of the ring is filled to the inside edge (fig. 18E).
6.   Finish off by taking the thread through the stitches to the back and to the centre before fastening off.
N.B. A variation can be made by dividing the spokes into groups and weaving each group separately to form a Maltese cross (figs. 18F and G).

Gardening Apron *(colour plate 8 and figs. 19 and 20)*

This gardening apron can be divided into several parts for a group project.

MATERIALS

127 cm (50 in.) of strong washable fabric 114 cm (45 in.) wide (sailcloth, denim, etc.)
Washable fabric pieces for appliqué motifs
Embroidery threads
Iron-on Vilene

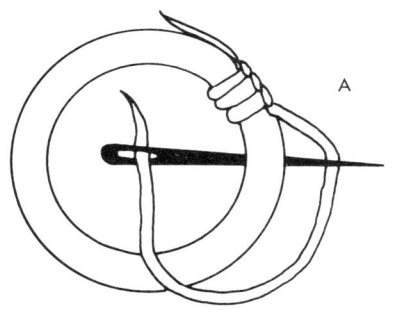

A

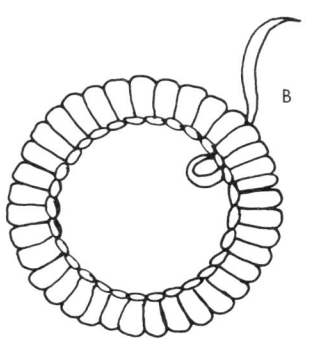

B

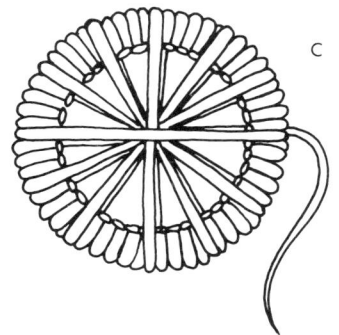

C

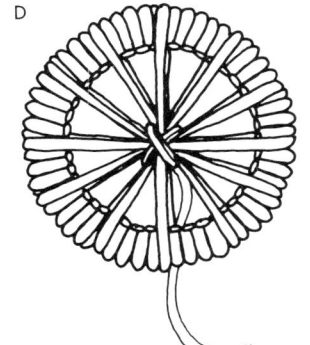

D

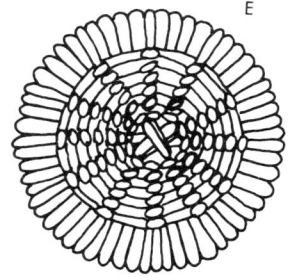

E

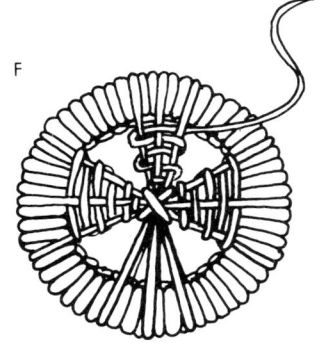

F

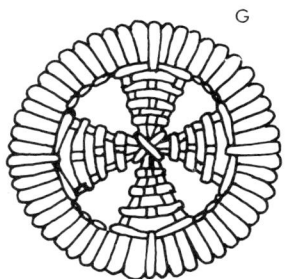

G

18.

METHOD

1. Cut out all sections of the apron as in fig. 19A.
2. Oversew all edges of the pockets to be embroidered to prevent fraying.
3. Cut out in card the basic shapes (circles, ovals, etc.) for templates for flower and vegetable motifs.
4. Trace or tack outlines of flowers etc. on pockets and apply appliqué motifs using iron-on Vilene.
5. With a machine, buttonhole or zigzag these motifs onto the pockets.
6. Embroider the motifs using simple stitches with suitable fabrics.

N.B. *Cauliflowers* can be suggested by using white towelling gathered into shape and held in place with random french knots.

Chrysanthemums are effective when worked in random detached chain using threads of various yellows and creams.

Marigolds can be shown by groups of buttonhole stitches with gaps showing the fabric beneath.

Leaves are best with shapes of green fabrics with simple stitches round the edges.

ASSEMBLING THE APRON

1. Tack and machine turnings on the apron skirt leaving one long side incomplete to be gathered into the waistband later.
2. Machine two small pockets to two large pockets making single units and apply each to the skirt (fig. 19B).
3. Tack and machine three sides of the bib and machine on the third small pocket (fig. 19C).
4. Tack turnings on the two waistband sections.
5. Gather the top of the skirt section and tack to the lower edge of one of the waistband sections.
6. Tack the bib section to the top of the waistband.
7. Make two strips of fabric 15 cm x 3 cm (6 in. x 1½ in.) into loops and stitch to the two upper corners of the waistband.
8. Apply the second waistband section, enclosing all raw edges and machine together.
9. Make two long ties 14 cm x 8 cm (45 in. x 3 in.) and sew to the top corners of the bib, to be taken over the shoulders, crossed at the back, threaded through loops and tied at the centre back.

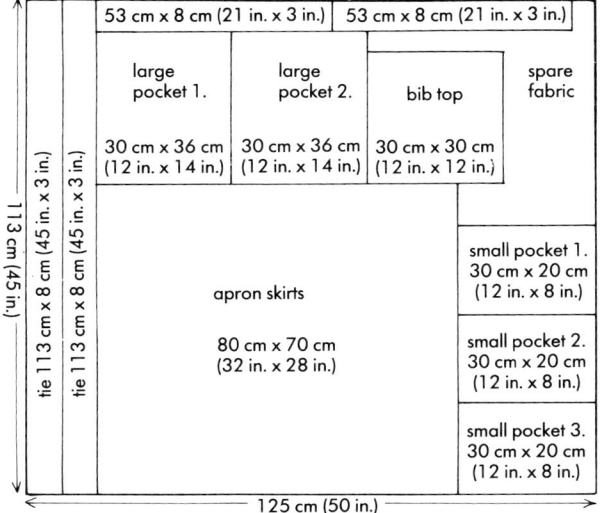

A

53 cm x 8 cm (21 in. x 3 in.) | 53 cm x 8 cm (21 in. x 3 in.)

tie 113 cm x 8 cm (45 in. x 3 in.)
tie 113 cm x 8 cm (45 in. x 3 in.)

113 cm (45 in.)

large pocket 1.

30 cm x 36 cm (12 in. x 14 in.)

large pocket 2.

30 cm x 36 cm (12 in. x 14 in.)

bib top

30 cm x 30 cm (12 in. x 12 in.)

spare fabric

apron skirts

80 cm x 70 cm (32 in. x 28 in.)

small pocket 1.
30 cm x 20 cm (12 in. x 8 in.)

small pocket 2.
30 cm x 20 cm (12 in. x 8 in.)

small pocket 3.
30 cm x 20 cm (12 in. x 8 in.)

125 cm (50 in.)

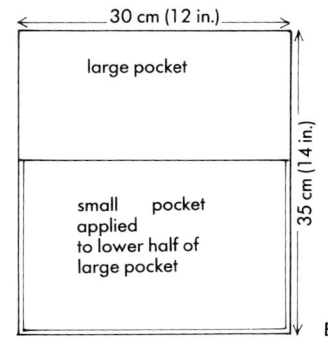

30 cm (12 in.)

large pocket

small pocket applied to lower half of large pocket

35 cm (14 in.)

B

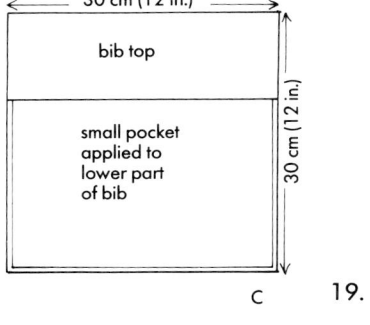

30 cm (12 in.)

bib top

small pocket applied to lower part of bib

30 cm (12 in.)

C

19.

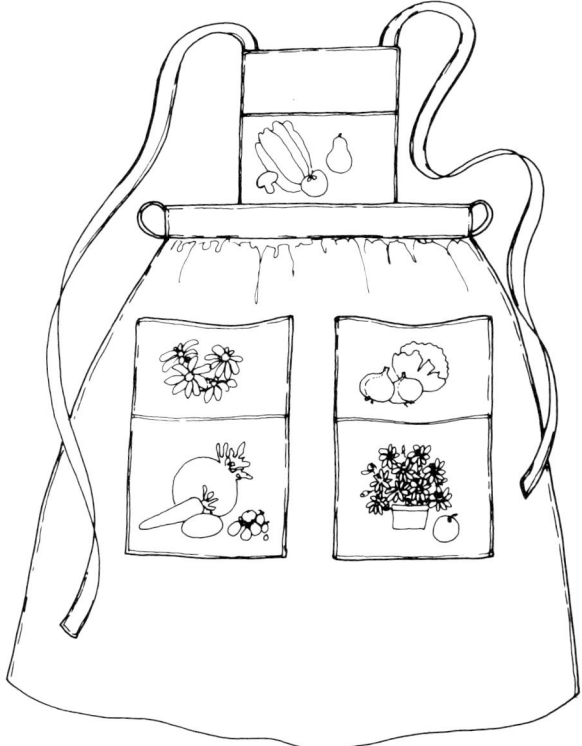

20.

29

Section Three

Animals in Patchwork Squares
(washable) *(colour plate 9 and fig. 21)*

Using square patches most animal shapes can be stylized to make a toy. The size of the squares determines the size of the toys, from life size to the tiny mobile family of dogs illustrated. All fabrics used should be washable and of the same weight and texture. Stretch fabrics are not satisfactory.

MATERIALS

Odd pieces of fabric in harmonising colours
Paper for templates
Pieces of foam rubber (or polyester wadding if preferred), the appropriate size and thickness for the stuffing.

METHOD

The *dog* requires 92 squares – 30 for each of the body sides and 32 for the joining strip (fig. 21A). The *elephant* requires 126 squares – 44 for each of the body sides and 38 for the joining strip (fig. 21B). The *snake* can be made from any number of squares forming single cubes (six squares) or longer blocks before being joined together by a length of firm string, knotted between each section. Enough string should be left at each end to make a tongue and tail (fig. 21C).

1.   Cut out the required number of squares in paper.
2.   Allowing 6 mm (¼ in.) turnings all round, cut out the same number of fabric squares. Make up and join in strips following the diagram, for the sides of the body.
3.   Join the squares for the joining strip into one length and stitch to the two body pieces leaving a gap on the underside for the stuffing.
4.   Cut a shape from the foam or wadding slightly larger than the pattern so that it fills the patchwork.
5.   Sew up the gap and decorate with features and extras as required.
N.B. The elephant is more effective if the forehead and tail end can be sewn back into triangles as indicated (fig. 21B). This will need some adjustment when sewing on the strip so that the squares fit accurately for the rest of the body pieces.

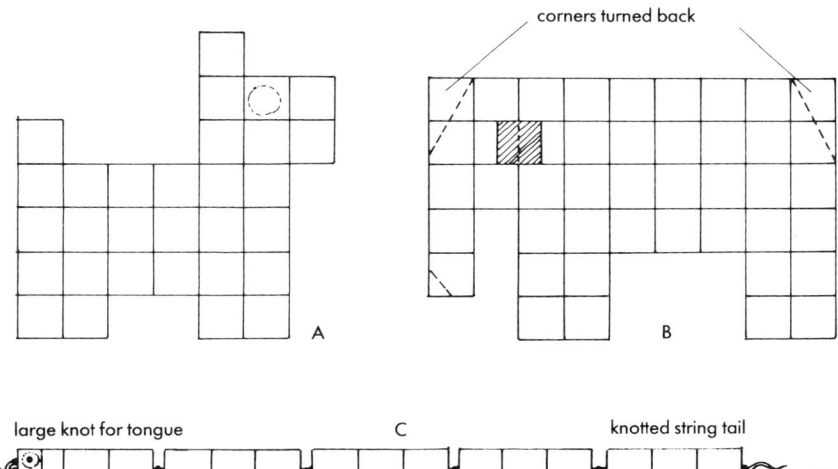

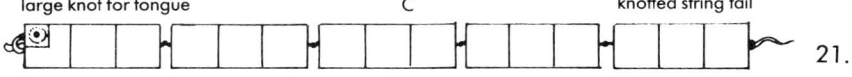

large knot for tongue   C   knotted string tail

21.

Patchwork Clown (washable)

(colour plate 10 and fig. 22)

MATERIALS

Odd pieces of fabric, white and striped
Wool for hair
Felt for feet
Paper for templates
Polyester wadding

METHOD

1. Cut 16 diamond-shaped paper templates measuring 10 cm x 8 cm (4 in. x 3 in.) along each axis (fig. 22A).
2. Allowing 6 mm (¼ in.) turnings, cut in fabric:
   six white diamonds
   six vertically striped diamonds
   four horizontally striped diamonds
3. Cover the paper templates with the fabric as in ordinary patchwork, and stitch together forming a pattern as in fig. 22B, leaving an opening at the top.
4. Turn inside out and stuff lightly with polyester wadding and sew up the head opening.
5. Embroider the face on one side of the head and cover the back and top of the head with wool to suggest hair.
6. Attach black felt triangles to the vertically striped 'legs' for feet and a bow tie in felt at the neck.
7. A string may be threaded through the head to make a hanging toy.

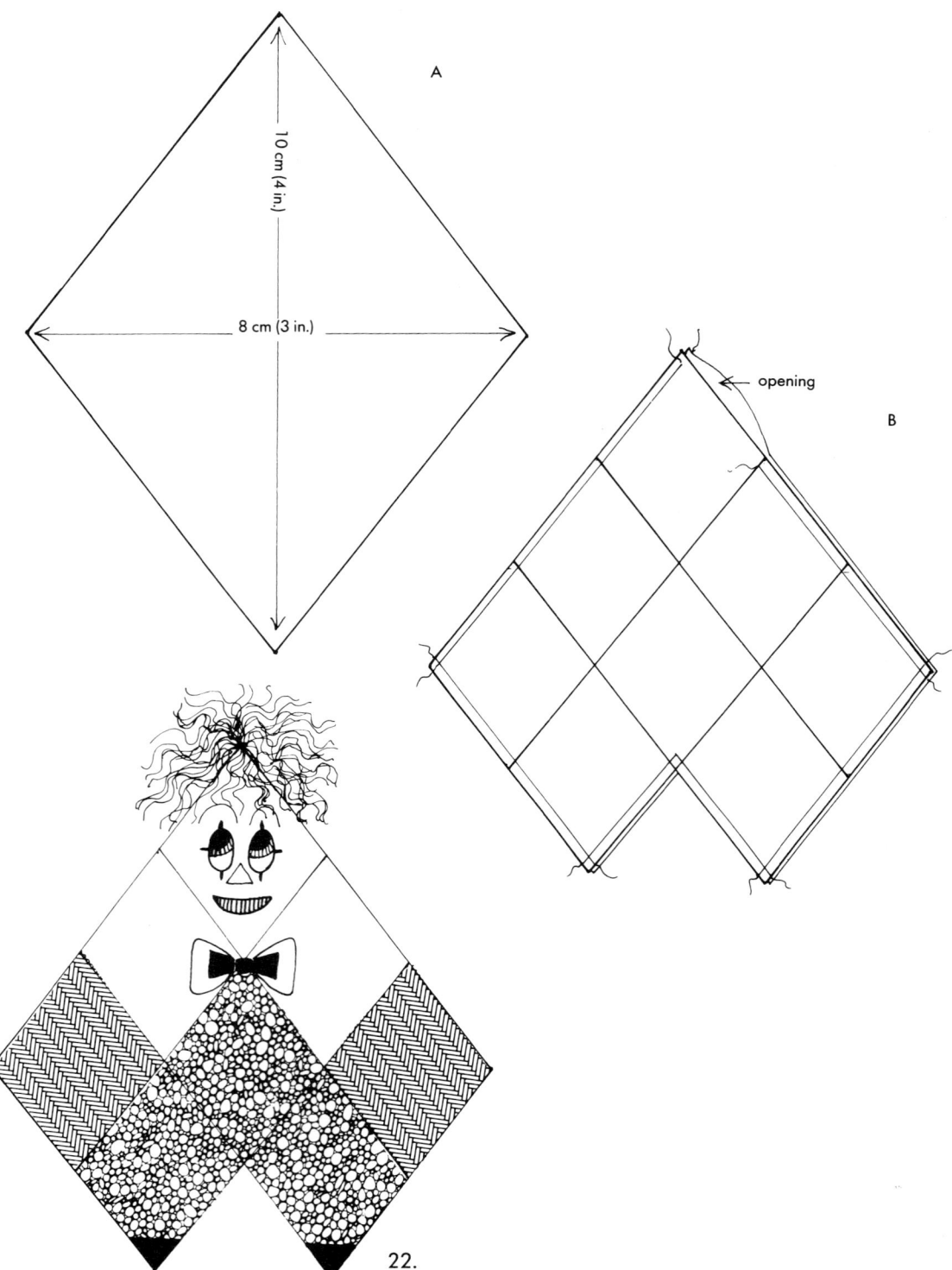

A

10 cm (4 in.)

8 cm (3 in.)

B

opening

22.

A Jumping Clown *(colour plate 10)*

This clown is made from Suffolk puffs which can be made from circles of fabric stuffed with wadding or cut directly from patterned polyester wadding fabric.

MATERIALS

Oddments of patterned polyester wadding fabric
91 cm (1 yd) of fine elastic (circular is best)
Odd pieces of felt and wool for hair, face features, hands and feet
Pieces of white felt and wool for the head
1 x 5 cm (2 in) diameter polystyrene ball from a florist
Thin card

METHOD

1. Draw a 13 cm (5 in.) diameter and a 9 cm (3½ in.) diameter circle in thin card.
2. From these templates, cut 11 x 13 cm (5 in.) diameter circles in fabric for the body, 9 x 9 cm (3½ in.) circles for each arm and 12 x 9 cm (3½ in.) circles for each leg.
3. Gather each circle of fabric into a 'puff' with large running stitches, 1 cm (⅜ in.) from edge (fig. 23A). Flatten and take one or two stitches across the centre to the sides to hold in place (fig. 23B).

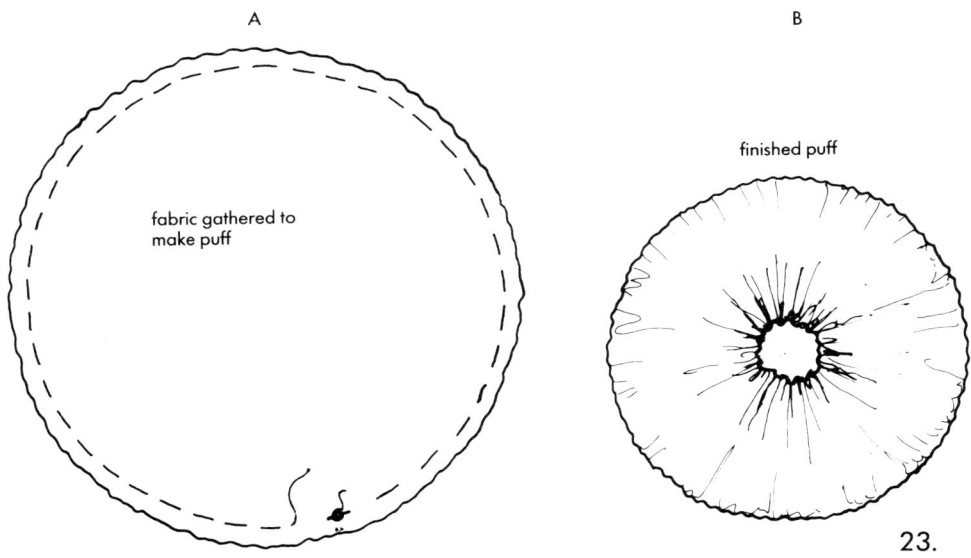

A

fabric gathered to
make puff

B

finished puff

23.

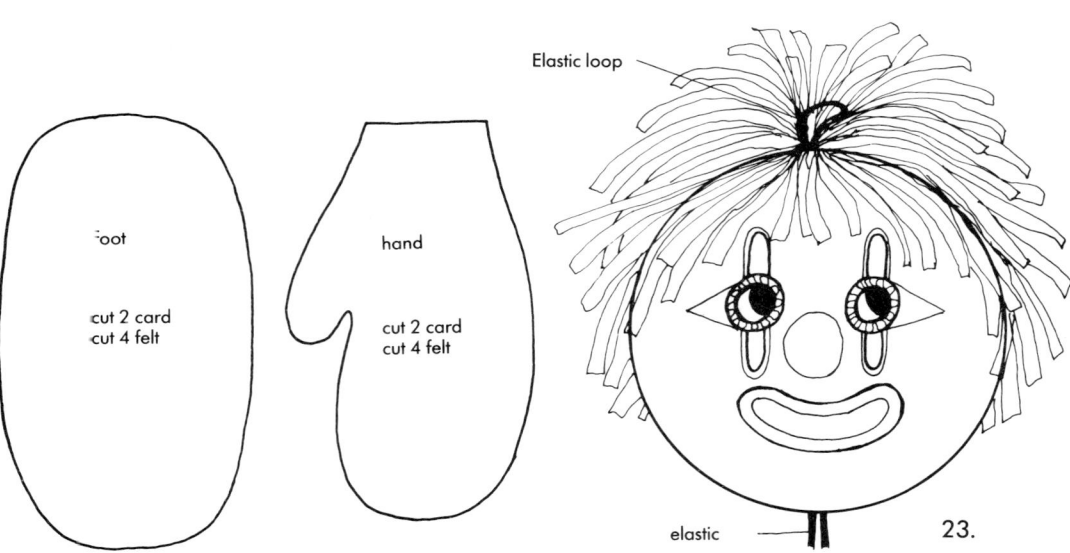

C.   D.   E.

foot

cut 2 card
cut 4 felt

hand

cut 2 card
cut 4 felt

Elastic loop

elastic   23.

4. For the legs, make a knot in the elastic and with a large-eyed needle thread the elastic through the centre of each of the 12 puffs so that both legs are in a continuous line on one piece of elastic. Knot the end and cut the elastic.

5. Treat the arms in the same way.

6. Join the body puffs in the same way but start at the bottom, leaving an end of elastic; turn at the top and return to the bottom. Knot the two ends of the elastic.

N.B. It is best to ensure that the untidy side of the puffs face each other at both ends of body, legs and arms.

7. Sew the knot at the base of the body to the centre of the elastic threaded through the legs.

8. Join the loop at the top of the body to the centre of the elastic threaded through the arms.

9. Make the head by covering the polystyrene ball with a tube made from the white felt, gathering or pleating it at the neck and top.

10. Embroider or attach ready-made felt features to the head (fig. 23E). Cover with wool for hair. (Two large puffs joined together will make a hat).

11. Join the head to the body by threading a piece of elastic through the loop at the top of the body and taking the two ends of elastic through the polystyrene head, hair and hat (with a long needle or fine crochet hook) leaving a loop long enough to put a finger through to manipulate the finished clown.

12. Cut out two card shapes for each of the hands and feet (fig. 23C and D). Cover with felt and oversew round the edges and attach to the arms and legs.

Section Four

Standing Alphabet _(colour plate 11 and fig. 24)_

A beautiful present for a child which could become a family heirloom.

MATERIALS

26 pieces of mounting card 9 cm x 11 cm (3½ in. x 4½ in.)
26 pieces of plain coloured cotton fabric in two toning colours
137 cm (1½ yds) of 3 cm (1 in.) corded ribbon to tone with fabrics
Oddments of felt and embroidery threads
15 cm (6 in.) elastic 1 cm (½ in.) wide
Length of thin fabric to make an elasticated band which holds the alphabet
strip when folded (fig. 24C).

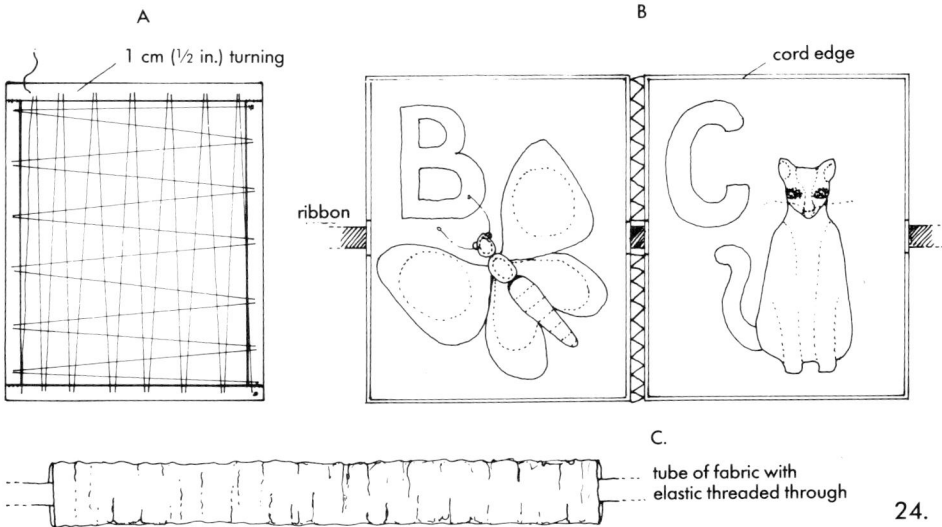

A

1 cm (½ in.) turning

B

cord edge

ribbon

C.

tube of fabric with
elastic threaded through

24.

METHOD

1. Draw an oblong 9 cm x 11 cm (3½ in. x 4½ in.) on each piece of fabric leaving 1 cm (½ in.) margins all round.
2. Cut out alphabet letters in felt about 5 cm (2 in.) high.
3. Decide on a motif for each letter (fig. 25.) and embroider it within and to one side of the oblong.
4. Position the felt letters to 'connect' to the embroidered motif and stitch on decoratively.
5. Turn the fabric edges over the card and lace tightly (fig. 24A).
6. With wrong sides together oversew the fabric-covered cards together leaving a 3 cm (1 in.) gap in the middle of each side for the ribbon to be threaded. (Back A on to N, B on to O and so on so that when the alphabet stands up the letters are in order (fig. 24B).
7. With thin handmade twisted cord, cover the oversewing, tucking the ends into the side gaps (fig. 24B).
8. Thread the ribbon right through each double card leaving an equal length of ribbon between each card (sewing it when finished to each card-covering at the gap edge) (fig. 24B).
9. Roll over the surplus ribbon to form a stop at each end.
10. The completed alphabet can be stored in a box made to fit, as illustrated, or held together by an elasticated strip (fig. 24C).

Child's Animal Book *(colour plate 11 and fig. 26)*

MATERIALS

8 pieces of calico 20 cm x 24 cm (8 in. x 9½ in.)
8 pieces of pelmet Vilene 19 cm x 23 cm (7½ in. x 9 in.)
Drawings, tracings or templates of animals etc. to fit calico
2 x 30 cm (12 in.) lengths of tape to 'close' book

METHOD

1. Draw or trace the selected animals on to each piece of calico.
2. Embroider these with either appliqué or simple stitchery.
3. Place the pelmet Vilene on the wrong side of each panel and tack turnings of 1 cm (½ in.) all round.
4. Arrange the panels in pairs, with the wrong sides together. Slip stitch round each panel to form four two-sided pieces.
5. Join these four panels together into one length of four double-sided panels, by slip stitching.
6. Attach tapes to tie the book when closed.

25. Suggested motifs for child's animal book and standing alphabet

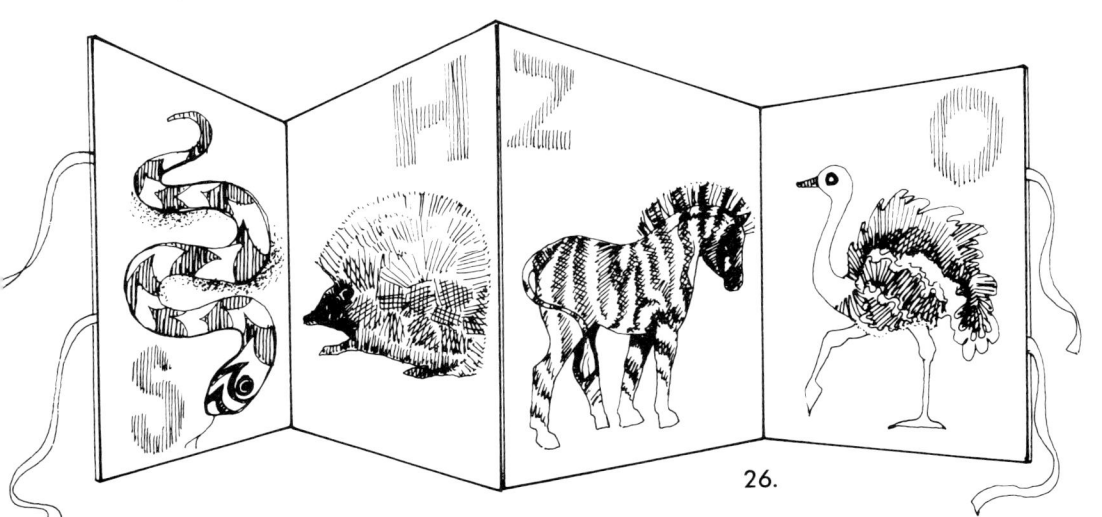

26.

Pram or Cot Quilts
(colour plate 12 and figs. 27 and 28)

Usually the word 'quilt' brings to mind the huge patchwork covers which takes many months to complete and which later become family heirlooms. Pram and cot quilts can also be made in the usual kinds of patchwork, however the illustration shows quilts made by several people, each working a 15 cm (6 in.) square which was applied to a piece of toning fabric and then backed and quilted. An advantage of this method is that the set of squares can suggest a theme to interest the child or its parents.

MATERIALS

2 pieces of fabric 76 cm x 53 cm (2 ft. 6 in. x 1 ft. 9 in.)
1 piece of polyester wadding 56 g (2 oz weight) 7 cm x 5 cm (2 ft. 5 in. x 1 ft. 8 in.)
12 x 15 cm (6 in.) squares of contrasting fabric for the motifs
Embroidery threads

METHOD

1. Draw or trace on to each square a motif to occupy most of the space, such as the stylized bird in figs. 27 and 28A, or butterflies, flowers, animals, etc.
2. Embroider these motifs (simple chain stitches and buttonhole variations were used in the illustration).
3. Fold in 1 cm (½ in.) turnings all round each square and tack all 12 squares into position on the right side of one of the large pieces of fabric.
4. Apply these pieces either by herringbone stitch or by zigzag machining (fig. 28B)
Either
5. Tack the polyester wadding on to the wrong side of the second piece of fabric and place over the finished appliquéd piece, the right side of the material to the right side of the work.
6. Machine all round 1 cm (½ in.) from the edge, leaving a 15 cm (6 in.) gap at the base for turning inside out.
7. Turn inside out, poke out the corners and slip stitch along the opening and press.
8. Stitch all round on the right side 0.5 cm (¼ in.) from the edge to make firm.
Or
5. Fold in 1 cm (½ in.) turning all round the edges of the appliquéd top and backing.
6. Place wadding between top and backing fabric and tack together.
7. Stitch all round quilt 1 cm (½ in.) from the edge.

To finish, machine right through all three layers each way between each applied square to form a quilt (fig. 28B).

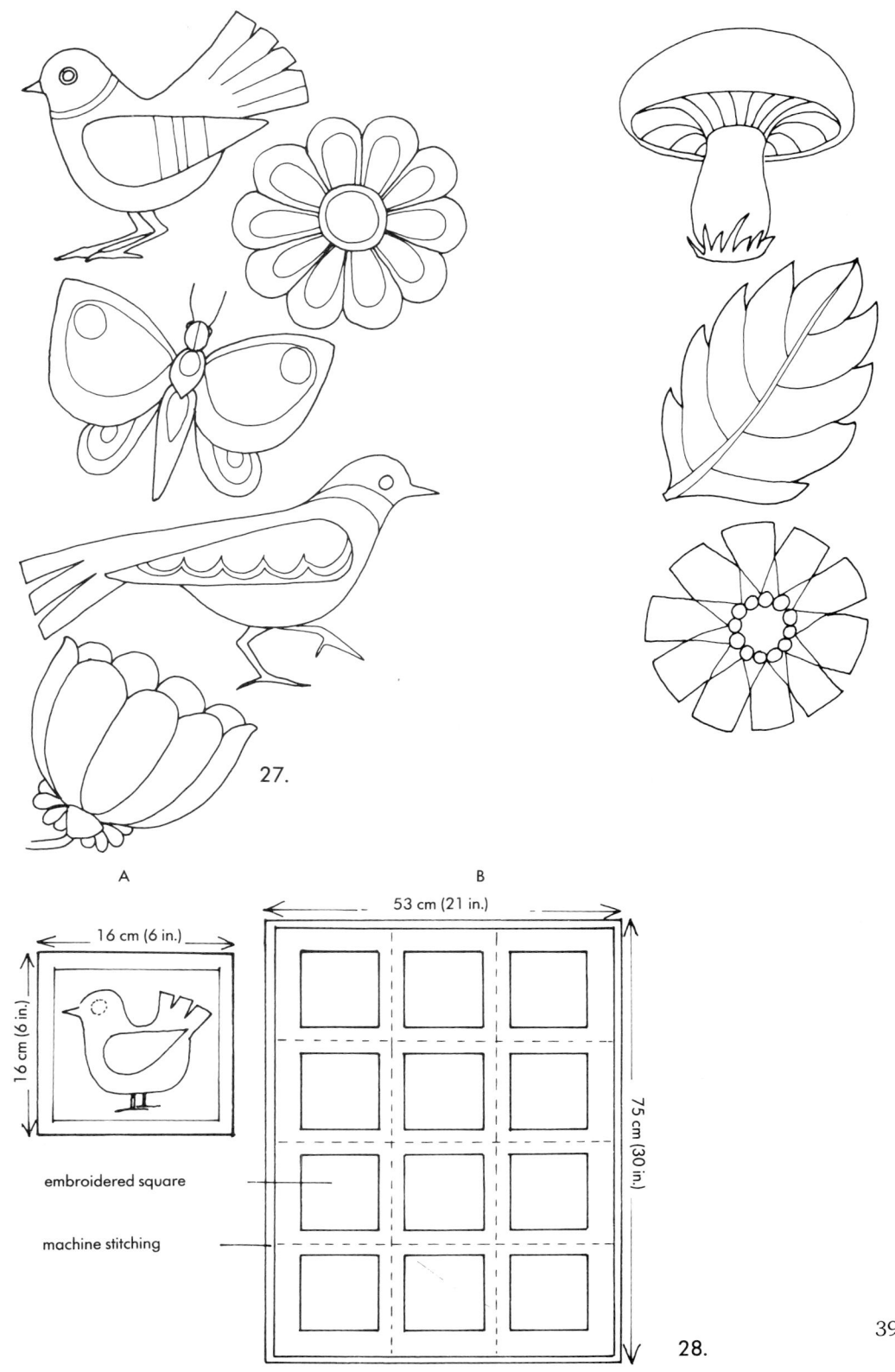

27.

A

B

16 cm (6 in.)

16 cm (6 in.)

53 cm (21 in.)

75 cm (30 in.)

embroidered square

machine stitching

28.

Child's Measuring Chart
(colour plate 13 and figs. 29, 30 and 31)

This design is fun for a child and a useful guide for its progressing height. It is based on the traditional rhyme:

> *Monday's child is fair of face,*
> *Tuesday's child is full of grace.*
> *Wednesday's child is full of woe,*
> *Thursday's child has far to go.*
> *Friday's child is loving and giving,*
> *Saturday's child work hard for its living.*
> *But the child who is born on the Sabbath Day,*
> *Is bonny and blithe and good and gay.*

MATERIALS

173 cm x 36 cm (68 in. x 14 in.) of strong fabric such as denim or sailcloth
Either
163 cm x 30 cm (64 in. x 12 in.) of lining material and 163 cm x 30 cm (64 in. x 12 in.) of card
Or
163 cm x 30 cm (64 in. x 12 in.) of pelmet Vilene
152 cm (60 in.) tape measure
36 cm (14 in.) dowel rod for hanging
7 pieces of 15 cm x 20 cm (6 in. x 8 in.) linen or firm cotton for each panel
Scraps of fabric for appliqué and the decorations for each figure (scraps of iron-on Vilene to prevent fraying)
229 cm (2½ yds) seam binding
Card for figure templates
7 pieces of Vilene 13 cm x 18 cm (5 in. x 7 in.)

METHOD

1. Draw or trace a figure on the card to make a template (fig. 29).
2. Draw or tack round the template on each piece of panel fabric.
3. Embroider or appliqué the panels to represent each day of the week.
4. Mount each completed panel over a rectangle of Vilene 13 cm x 18 cm (5 in. x 7 in.).
5. Attach each panel to the backing fabric by hand or machine, leaving 3 cm (1¼ in.) between each panel and 10 cm (4 in.) at the bottom (fig. 30).
6. Make a 3 cm (1 in.) turning at the top. Fold down and stitch 5 cm (2 in.) from the fold to make a tube through which the dowel rod will be pushed (fig. 30).
7. Attach string or hooks at each end of the rod for hanging.
8. Apply the tape measure to the background either by stitching or by sticking (fig. 30).
9. Embroider or write the rhyme for each day on to lengths of seam binding and sew to the appropriate panels (fig. 30).
10. Turn in the 3 cm (1 in.) hem allowance round the two sides and bottom and back with either pelmet Vilene or card covered with material to add weight to the hanging.

29.

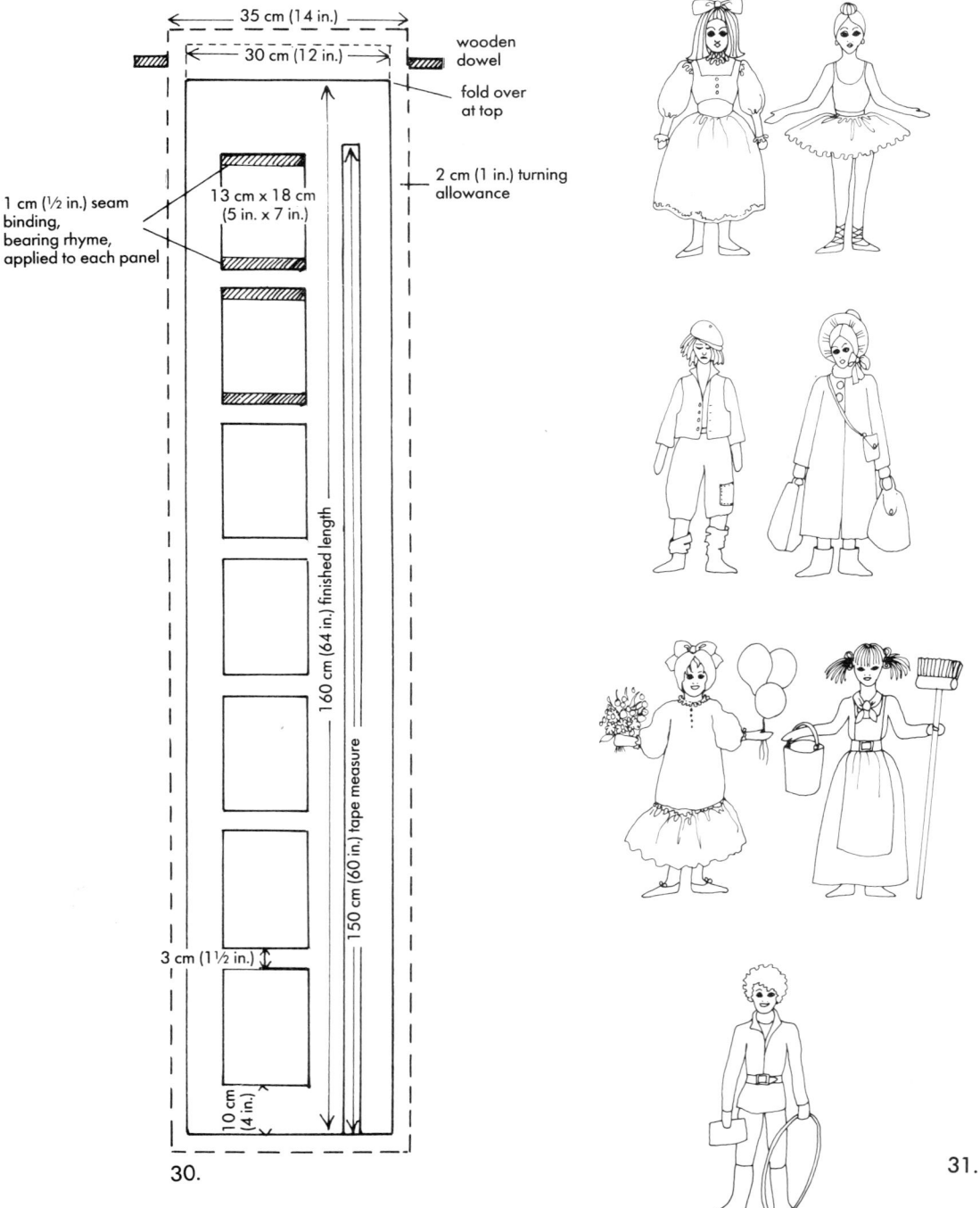

35 cm (14 in.)

30 cm (12 in.)

wooden dowel

fold over at top

2 cm (1 in.) turning allowance

1 cm (½ in.) seam binding, bearing rhyme, applied to each panel

13 cm x 18 cm (5 in. x 7 in.)

160 cm (64 in.) finished length

150 cm (60 in.) tape measure

3 cm (1½ in.)

10 cm (4 in.)

30.

31.

Section Five

Finishings *(colour plate 7 and figs. 32 to 36)*

Cords, tassels or ties are needed when making up some of the articles in this book. The whole effect is enhanced if the finishings are handmade with colours to harmonise, or oddments of the original material are used.

SIMPLE TASSELS

1. Cut a piece of card the required depth of the tassel, and around this wind the wood or thread 40 or 50 times (fig. 32A).
2. Cut the threads along one edge of the card, and whilst the threads are still folded in half, pass a looped thread round the group of threads at the middle. This loop holds the threads together whilst the tassel is being made (fig. 32B).
3. Pad the head of the tassel with a small wad of cottonwool or oddments of wool and secure it with a looped thread. Take this thread up through the padding to the top of the tassel and leave the end to be used later for attaching the tassel. It may also be left as in fig. 32C.
4. Decorate by covering the head with detached buttonhole stitch, beginning at the top and working round in circles until the securing thread at the base of the tassel is reached (fig. 32D).
5. Trim the ends of the tassel.
N.B. If enough thread is left through the top of the tassel, beads and knots can be added as further decoration (fig. 32E).

FELT OR MATERIAL TASSEL 5 cm (2 in.) DEEP *(fig. 33)*

1. Cut a piece of felt or material 15 cm x 5 cm (6 in. x 2 in.) and snip a fringe 3 cm (1 in.) deep the length of the felt (fig. 33A).
2. Stitch a looped thread at one top end and roll the material tightly round this to the end. Stitch right through to secure.

3. Wrap a thread round 1 cm (½ in.) from the top to bind (fig. 33).
4. With the fingers open up the fringed edge.
N.B. If material is used, unusual effects can be obtained if a line of stitching is done approximately 3 cm (1 in.) from the bottom and the weft threads of the material drawn out to this line.

A SIMPLE BOBBLE *(fig. 33)*

1. Cut two circles of card 3 cm (1 in.) radius and cut a hole 1.5 cm (½ in.) across at the centre.
2. Wrap wool evenly through the hole and over the edges of both cards until the card is covered and the hole tightly filled (fig. 33C).
3. Cut the wool at the outer edges between the cards and pull the cards apart a little.
4. Slip a tying thread between the cards and tie securely.
5. Remove both pieces of card, fluff out the wool and trim the bobble to shape.

A TWISTED CORD *(fig. 34)*

Cords can be made to any thickness, by increasing the thickness and number of threads.
1. Cut the threads three times the length of the cord required.
2. Knot a loop at each end and slip one loop over a hook.
3. Slip a pencil into the other loop, stretch the thread taut and twist the pencil continually in the same direction until it becomes tight and begins to curl.
4. Take hold of the centre and take the pencil end to the hook.
5. Hold both ends and release the cord hand and it will twist automatically into a cord. This is easier if you can hang a weight at the middle.
6. Smooth out evenly.

A FINGER CORD *(fig. 35)*

1. Take two different coloured threads X and Y.
2. Knot the two together and work upwards, making a loop first with X and then with Y.
3. Insert loop X into loop Y.
4. Pull loop Y tightly and make another loop through X.
5. Pull loop X tightly and make a loop through Y.
6. Continue until the required length is made.

A PLAITED CORD *(fig. 36)*

1. Take three (or a multiple of three) threads of the required length of cord.
2. Tie together and place over a hook.
3. Separate the threads and take the left-hand one over the thread immediately to its right.
4. Take the right-hand thread and pass over the thread immediately to its left.
5. Take the left-hand thread and pass over the right-hand thread as before.
6. Take the right-hand thread and pass over the left-hand thread as before. Continue until the plait is finished.

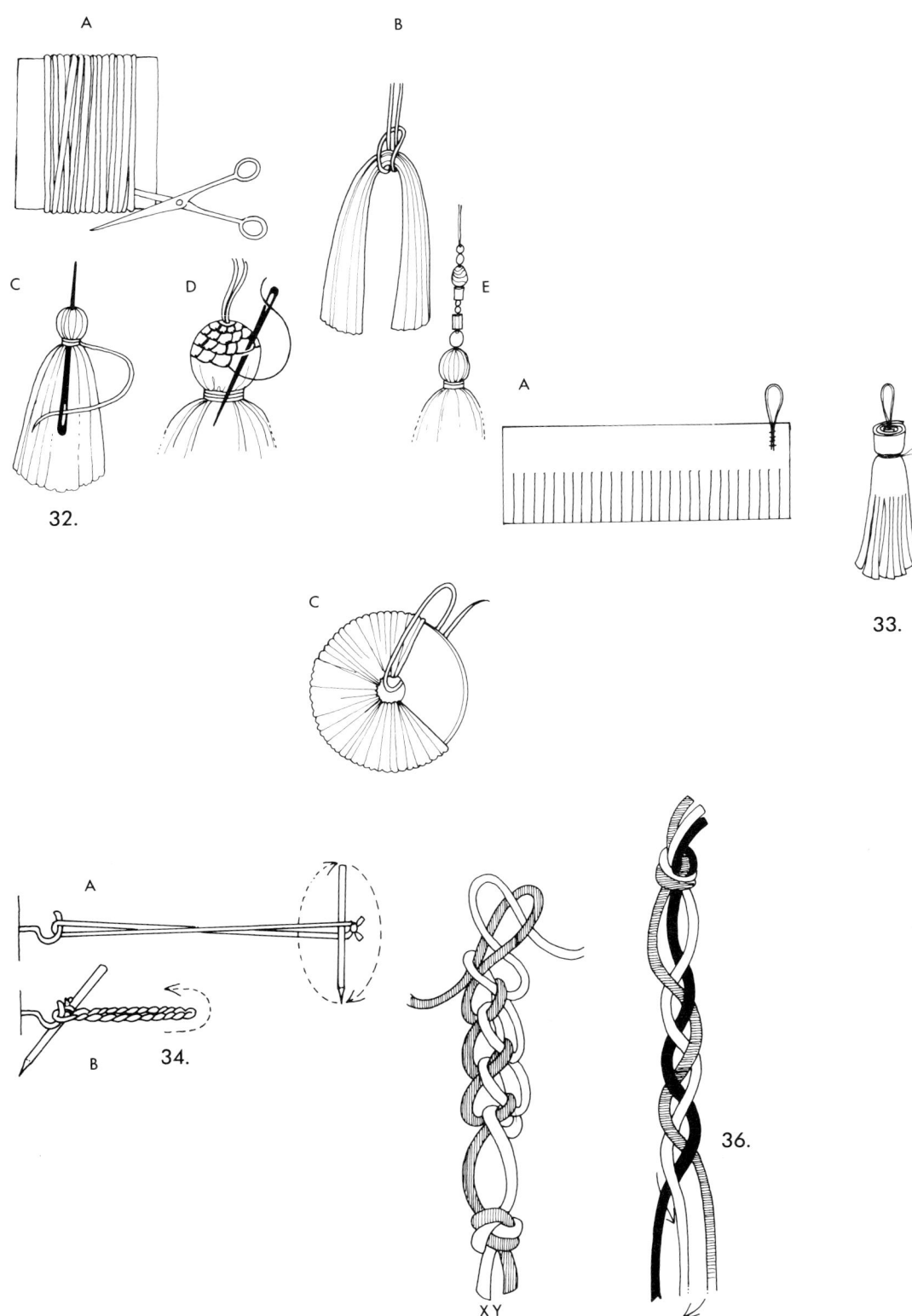

A

B

C

D

E

32.

A

B

33.

C

A

B

34.

35.

X Y

36.

Bibliography

As the introduction to this book indicates, no teaching of techniques is given. The following books will be found to be very helpful.

BEANEY, JAN	*Stitches: New Approaches*	B. T. Batsford
BEANEY, JAN	*Embroidery: New Approaches*	Pelham Books
BUTLER, ANNE	*Batsford Encyclopaedia of Embroidery Stitches*	B. T. Batsford
BUTLER, ANNE	*Simple Stitches*	B. T. Batsford
B.B.C. PUBLICATIONS	*Discovering Patchwork*	
GOSTELOW, MARY	*Blackwork*	B. T. Batsford
GRAY, JENNIFER	*Canvas Work*	B. T. Batsford
GREEN, SYLVIA	*Canvas Embroidery for Beginners*	Studio Vista
GEDDES, ELISABETH AND MOYRA McNEILL	*Blackwork Embroidery*	Dover
LILEY, ALISON	*The Craft of Embroidery*	Mills & Boon
PHILLPOTT, PAT	*The Craft of Embroidery*	Stanley Paul
PYMAN, KIT (Editor)	*Needlecraft Series*	Search Press
RHODES, MARY	*Needlepoint*	Cathay Books
RUSSELL, PAT	*Lettering for Embroidery*	B. T. Batsford
SNOOK, BARBARA	*Embroidery Stitches*	Dryad Press
SNOOK, BARBARA	*Learning to Embroider*	B. T. Batsford
WARK, EDNA	*The Craft of Patchwork*	B. T. Batsford

Suppliers

UK

The Campden Needlecraft Centre, High Street, Chipping Campden, Gloucestershire
S. N. Cooke Ltd., 18 Wood Street, Stratford-on-Avon, Warwickshire
The Handicraft Shop, 5 Oxford Road, Altrincham, Cheshire
The Handworker's Market, 6 Bull Street, Holt, Norfolk NR25 6HP
Mace and Nairn, 8 Crane Street, Salisbury, Wiltshire SP1 2PY
Needle and Thread, 80 High Street, Horsell, Woking, Surrey
The Nimble Thimble, 26 The Green, Bilton, Rugby CV22 7LY
Richmond Art and Craft, Dept. E1, 181 City Road, Cardiff CF2 3JB
Christine Riley, 53 Barclay Street, Stonehaven, Kincardineshire AB3 2AR
Royal School of Needlework, 25 Princes Gate, London SW7 1QE
Spinning Jenny, Bradley, Keighley, West Yorkshire BD20 9DD
Teazle Embroideries, 35 Boothferry Road, Hull HU3 6UA

USA

Appleton Brothers of London, West Main Road, Little Compton, Rhode Island 02837
American Crewel Studio, Box 298, Boonton, New Jersey 07005
American Thread Corporation, 90 Park Avenue, New York
Bucky King Embroideries, Box 371, King Bros, 3 Ranch Buffalo Star Rte, Sheridan, Wyoming 82801
Craft Kaleidoscope, 6412 Ferguson Street, Indianapolis 46220
Dharma Trading Company, 1952 University Avenue, Berkeley, California 94704
The Golden Eye, Box 205, Chestnut Hill, Massachusetts 02167
Heads and Tails, River Forest, Illinois 60305
Lily Mills, Selby, North Carolina 28150
Threadbenders, 2260 Como Avenue, St. Paul, Minnesota 55108
The Thread Shed, 307 Freeport Road, Pittsburgh, Pennsylvania 15215